San Die...e

San Diego, Cal...

By Christopher D. London

TEMPLE ☐ BRICKS

San Diego California Temple
San Diego, California, USA

TEMPLE FACTS

Number: .... 47th constructed, 45th operating

Announcement: ..... 7 April 1984

Groundbreaking: ... 27 February 1988 by Ezra Taft Benson

Open House: .... 20 February - 3 April 1993

Dedication: .... 25 April 1993 by Gordon B. Hinckley

Site: .... 7.2 acres (2.9 ha)

Exterior Finish: ...... Marble chips in plaster

Rooms: .... Four ordinance (stationary)

Eight sealing

Total Floor Area: .... 72,000 square feet (6,700 m²)

Height: .... 169 feet (52 m)

HISTORY

The San Diego California Temple was the third temple built in California, following the Los Angeles California Temple (1956) and the Oakland California Temple (1964). It is the 47th constructed and 45th operating temple of The Church of Jesus Christ of Latter-day Saints.

After suffering a mild heart attack four months earlier, President Ezra Taft Benson made his first trip outside the Salt Lake Valley to break ground for the San Diego California Temple on 7 April 1984—his first time presiding over a temple groundbreaking.

On Monday, 23 December 1991, the 186th anniversary of the birth of the Prophet Joseph Smith, a gilded statue of the angel Moroni was installed atop the eastern spire of the San Diego California Temple. Shortly after the setting, a traveling flock of seagulls—a bird of symbolic significance to the Church—circled the new statue about three times before continuing on its course.

Over 720,000 visitors attended the widely publicized open house of the San Diego California Temple.

President Benson's ailing health did not allow him to preside at the dedication of the San Diego California Temple. President Gordon B. Hinckley was assigned to dedicate the temple in 23 sessions where 49,273 people attended.

ARCHITECTURE & DESIGN

The architects for the San Diego California Temple were William S. Lewis, Jr., design architect; Dennis Hyndman, project architect; and Shelly Hyndman, interior design architect. The Hyndmans, who are Roman Catholic, had not toured the interior of a Latter-day Saint temple until the Las Vegas Nevada Temple open house commenced in 1989.

The temple was designed with two main spires, but unique to this temple are four smaller spires at the base of each main spire. The east spire is topped with the familiar Angel Moroni statue which adorns most LDS temples.

Connecting the towers at the center is a supernal star-shaped atrium filled with a healthy, colorful garden. The atrium is accessed from the breathtaking two-story Celestial Room filled with towering art glass, suspended light fixtures, and features a grand staircase to an upper-level balcony.

The exterior finish is marble chips in stucco giving the building a white glow.

The temple is built on a 7.2-acre (2.9 hetacre) plot, has 4 ordinance rooms and 8 sealing rooms, and has a total floor area of 72,000 square feet (6,700 square meters).

HONORS & AWARDS

The San Diego California Temple was honored as Headliner of the Year for 1993 in the landmark category by the San Diego Press Club.

For its efforts during the open house of the San Diego California Temple to increase public awareness of the Church and the role of the temple, the Church was presented with the Public Relations Society of America's prestigious Silver Anvil Award in the category of special events and observances by non-profit organizations.

1

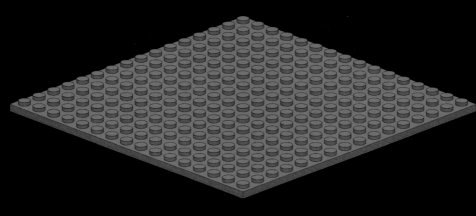

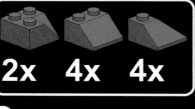

2x **4x** **4x**

2

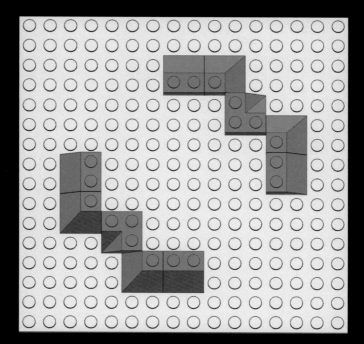

3

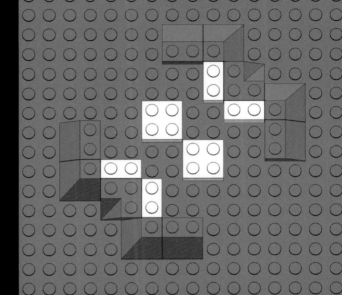

4

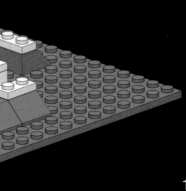

5

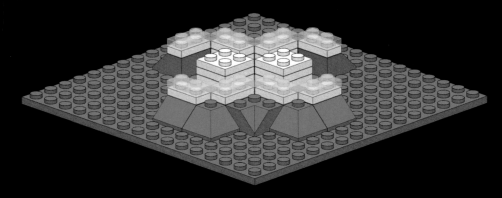

6

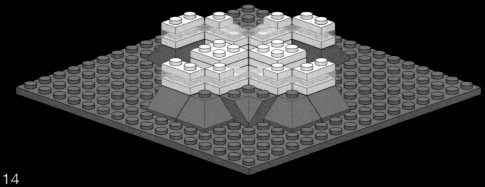

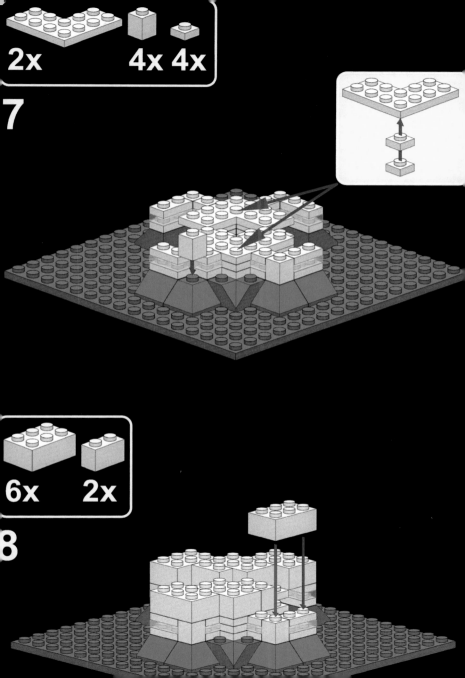

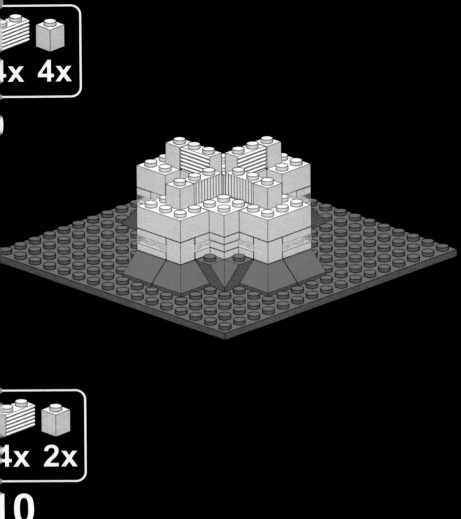

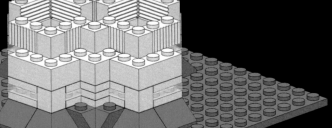

4x

11

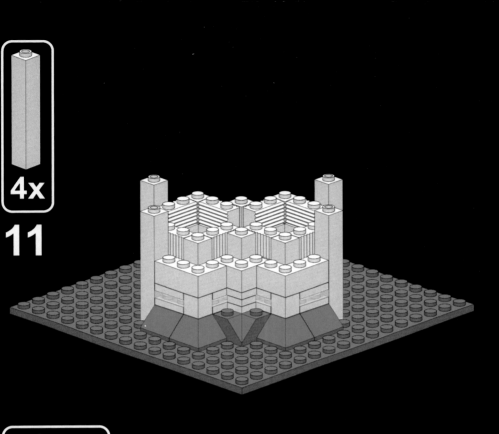

1x 9x

12

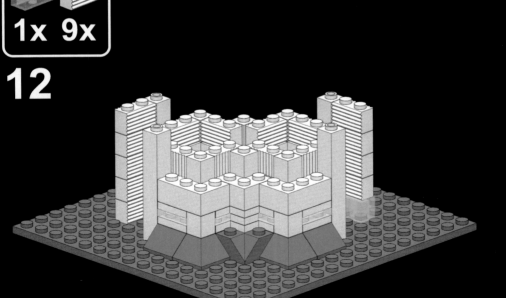

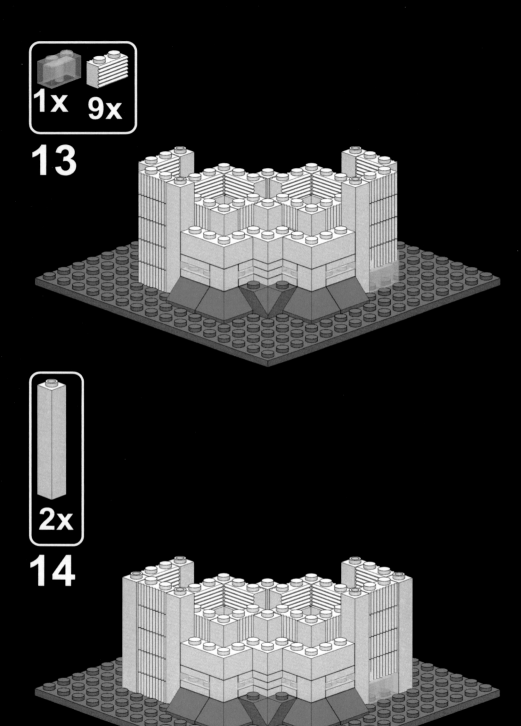

4x

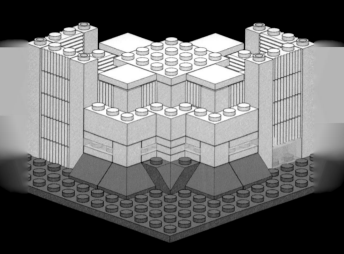

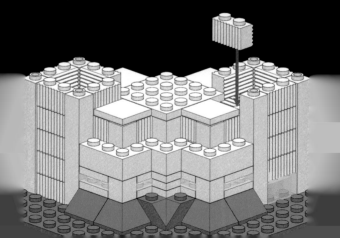

4x

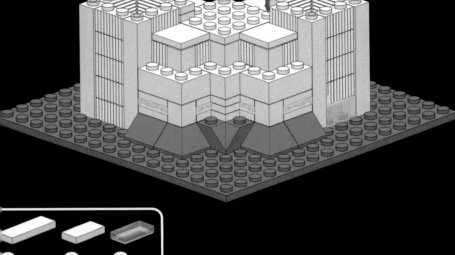

2x 2x 2x

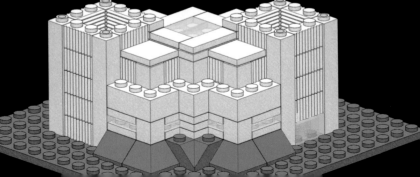

19

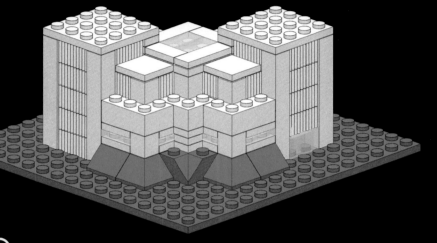

20

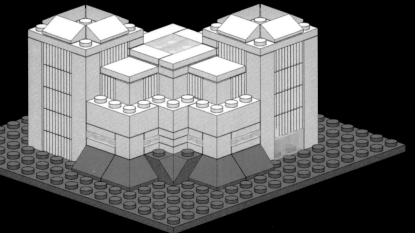

2x

21

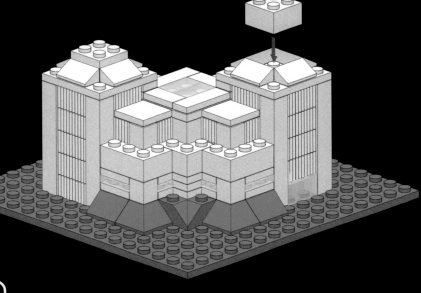

8x

22

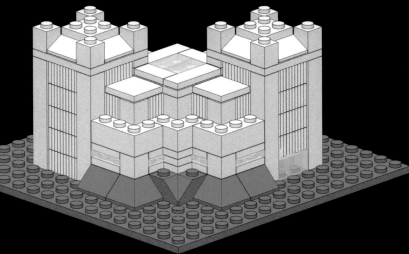

2x 8x

23

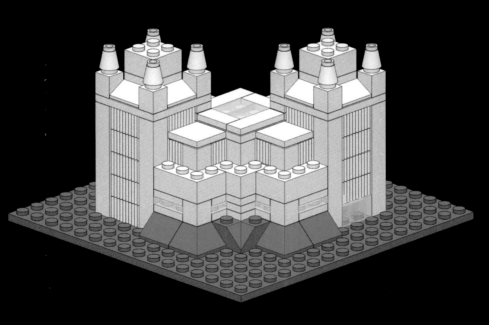

2x 2x

24

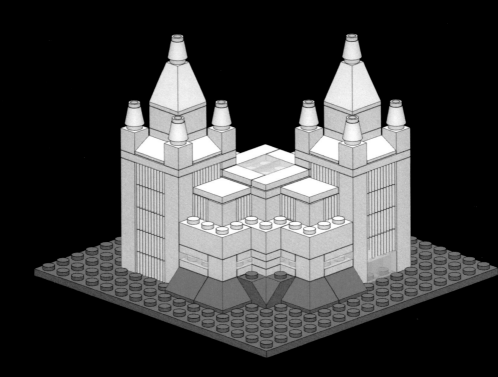

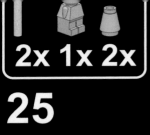

2x 1x 2x

25

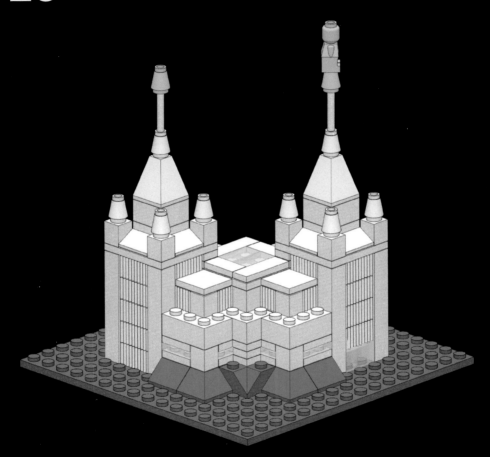

The San Diego California Temple is one of my personal favorites. As a child, I was able to enter the temple during the public open house making it the first time I have entered a temple of The Church of Jesus Christ of Latter-day Saints. I was awe-inspired by the majesty of such a magnificent structure.

Having been raised in the Los Angeles California Temple district, it seemed that attending the San Diego California Temple would be limited to proxy ordinances but when the time came for me to get my own endowments the Los Angeles California Temple was closed for cleaning and so I received my own endowments at the San Diego California Temple. Later on in my life I was sealed there to my best friend on the 143rd day of the year 2009.

With as much personal history as I have with this temple I felt it only fitting that it was the first temple I designed. I hope you have as much fun building this temple as I did designing it and hopefully the success of this instruction book will pave the way for more books just like it.

CHRISTOPHER DOUGLAS LONDON

ABOUT TEMPLE ⬚ BRICKS

The founder and CEO of Temple Bricks, Chris London, has always loved creative toys that help kids unplug from technology. In his continuing pursuit to find the best toys he realized that there is a lack of engaging toys for certain demographics, specifically within the LDS community. As an AFOL, he found the perfect match in toy bricks.

© David Steele

Not wanting to limit his toys to just the LDS community he started Temple Bricks as a way to create and design building toys for different religious and historical groups.

Temple Bricks officially started on 28 August 2013 with the purchase of the domain: TempleBricks.com. Other sister domains have also been purchased including Scripture-Bricks.com and LDSBricks.com. Since that time many temple models have been designed and await manufacturing.

The logo for Temple Bricks comes from the common religious symbol of the circle inside the square. The picture above is of the railing at the San Diego California Temple. The symbol, however, can be found in many cultures (with their own meaning) including Chinese, Japanese, Egyptian, Christian, and Muslim. The circle frequently refers to the eternal or the spiritual since a circle has no beginning or end. The square commonly refers to physical or temporal things such as the earth as in the saying "the four corners of the earth." We believe the symbol means "where the spiritual meets the temporal" or in the case of a religious building "Heaven on Earth."

We hope these toys bring new fun and excitement to your families as they have to ours.

LDS TEMPLE SERIES

San Diego California Temple
01001

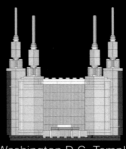

Washington D.C. Temple
01002

Mount Timpanogos Utah Temple
01003

Provo Utah Temple
01004

Mexico City Mexico Temple
01005

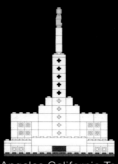

Los Angeles California Temple
01006

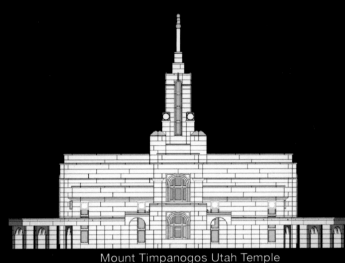

Mount Timpanogos Utah Temple
02003

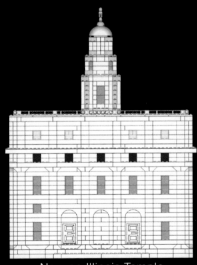

Nauvoo Illinois Temple
02007

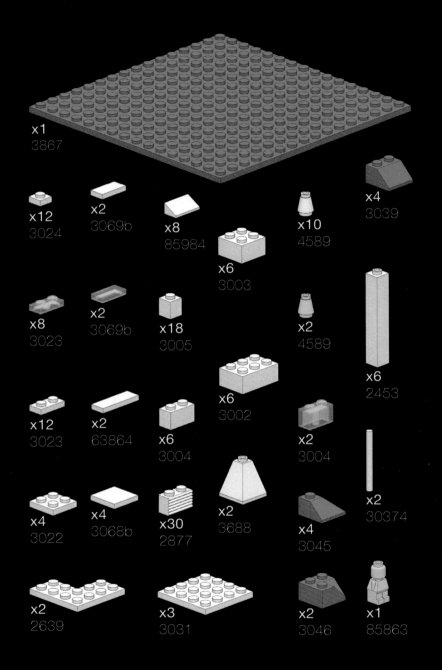

x1
3867

x12
3024

x2
3069b

x8
85984

x10
4589

x4
3039

x6
3003

x8
3023

x2
3069b

x18
3005

x2
4589

x6
2453

x12
3023

x2
63864

x6
3004

x6
3002

x2
3004

x4
3022

x4
3068b

x30
2877

x2
3688

x4
3045

x2
30374

x2
2639

x3
3031

x2
3046

x1
85863

Need pieces? See our buying guide at www.templebricks.com/where-to-buy

REFERENCES

Text

LDS Church Temples, all rights reserved.
www.ldschurchtemples.com

Wikipedia, CC BY-SA 3.0.
www.wikipedia.org

Photos

Christopher Douglas London, all rights reserved.
www.TempleBricks.com

Tyler Foote, all rights reserved.
www.TemplesByTyler.com

Antoine Taveneaux, CC BY-SA 3.0.
commons.wikimedia.org/wiki/User:Antoinetav

David Steele, CC BY 2.0.
www.flickr.com/photos/hombredesteele